U.S.A. TRAVEL GUIDES

RHODE ISLAND

BY ANN HEINRICHS • ILLUSTRATED BY MATT KANIA

The
Child's
World®
childsworld.com

Published by The Child's World®
1980 Lookout Drive • Mankato, MN 56003-1705
800-599-READ • www.childsworld.com

Photo Credits
Photographs ©: JJM Photography/Shutterstock Images,
cover, 1; iStockphoto, 7, 11, 19, 28, 31, 32; Conner Scott/
iStockphoto, 8; K.L. Kohn/Shutterstock Images, 12; Lee
Snider Photo Images/Shutterstock Images, 15; Marc
Dufresne/iStockphoto, 16; H.C. Williams CC2.0, 20;
Mary Terriberry/Shutterstock Images, 23; Glenn Price/
Shutterstock Images, 24; Dan Logan/iStockphoto, 27;
Shutterstock Images, 35, 37 (top), 37 (bottom)

ISBN 9781503819795
LCCN 2016961622

Printing
Printed in the United States of America
PA02334

Ann Heinrichs is the author
of more than 100 books
for children and young
adults. She has also enjoyed
successful careers as a
children's book editor and
an advertising copywriter.
Ann grew up in Fort Smith,
Arkansas, and lives in
Chicago, Illinois.

About the Author
Ann Heinrichs

Matt Kania loves maps and, as a
kid, dreamed of making them. In
school he studied geography and
cartography, and today he makes
maps for a living. Matt's favorite
thing about drawing maps is
learning about the places they
represent. Many of the maps
he has created can be found in
books, magazines, videos, Web
sites, and public places.

About the
Map Illustrator
Matt Kania

*On the cover: The Newport bridge is
in Jamestown, Rhode Island.*

OUR RHODE ISLAND TRIP

RHODE ISLAND

How about a trip through the Ocean State? That's Rhode Island! It may be a tiny state. But you'll find it's full of adventures.

You'll see the silliest boats you can imagine. You'll spot bushes shaped like animals. You'll sail through the air on a merry-go-round. You'll gaze up at lighthouses. And you'll see ocean waves crashing ashore.

How's that for an exciting ride? Now, settle in and buckle up tight. We're off to see Rhode Island!

WELCOME TO
RHODE ISLAND

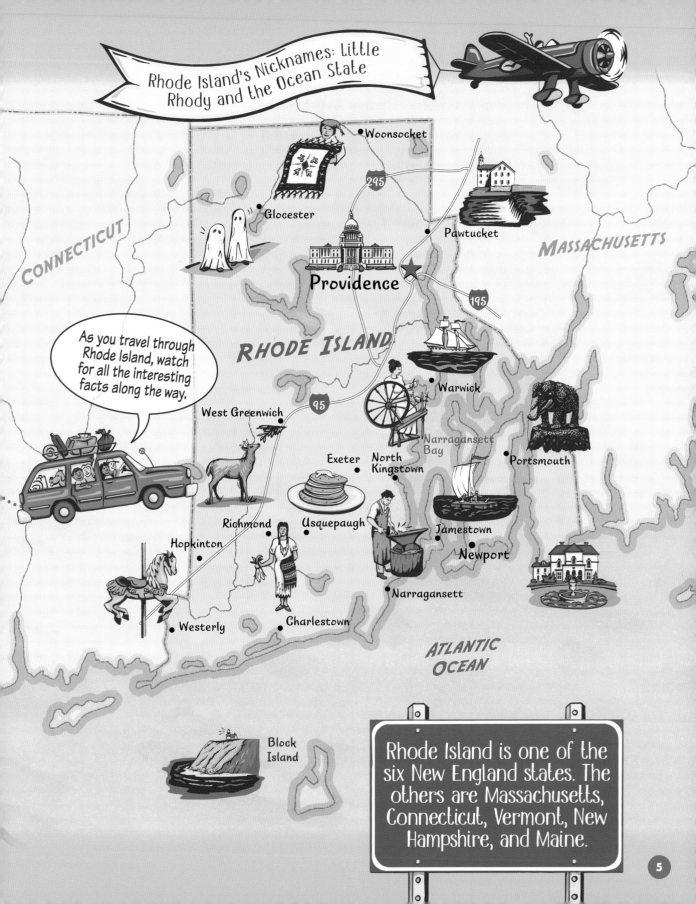

BLOCK ISLAND'S MOHEGAN BLUFFS

Stroll along Mohegan Bluffs on Block Island. Waves crash on the rocks far below you. Here and there, tall lighthouses rise. All around you are sweeping views of the sea.

Rhode Island is the smallest state. It has miles of coastline, though. Narragansett Bay almost cuts the state in two. This bay flows into the Atlantic Ocean. Some coastal areas are rocky. Others have sandy beaches.

Dozens of islands lie in the bay. The largest is Aquidneck Island. Next in size are Conanicut and Prudence islands. Block Island lies south of the **mainland**. From there, you see miles of ocean. No wonder Rhode Island is called the Ocean State!

Experience Rhode Island's natural beauty at Mohegan Bluffs.

ARCADIA WILDLIFE MANAGEMENT AREA

Sneak through the thick underbrush. You may spot a white-tailed deer. Do you hear rustling? It could be a raccoon or a mink. It might be a wild turkey or a pheasant. It could even be a little fox!

You're exploring Arcadia Wildlife Management Area. It's a wooded area in western Rhode Island. You'll see ponds, streams, and waterfalls there. It's a great home for forest animals.

You might spot cottontail rabbits and hawks. Gray squirrels and snowshoe hares live there, too. If you want to fish, head to Frosty Hollow Pond in Exeter. It's just for kids!

Enjoy the waterfalls at Stepstone Falls.

STATE FLOWER
VIOLET

STATE TREE
RED MAPLE

STATE BIRD
RHODE ISLAND RED

Let's find Stepstone Falls! We can take our shoes off and walk down the waterfall!

CONNECTICUT

MASSACHUSETTS

West Greenwich •

Arcadia Wildlife Management Area

• Exeter

Richmond •

• Kingston

• Hopkinton

The National Park Service has five sites in Rhode Island.

Arcadia Wildlife Management Area is spread over four towns. They are West Greenwich, Exeter, Hopkinton, and Richmond.

It's an old Rhode Island **tradition** to have a **clambake** on the beach.

Rhode Island's Great Swamp is near Kingston. Vines drape down from its trees. Kingfishers, ducks, and many other waterbirds live there.

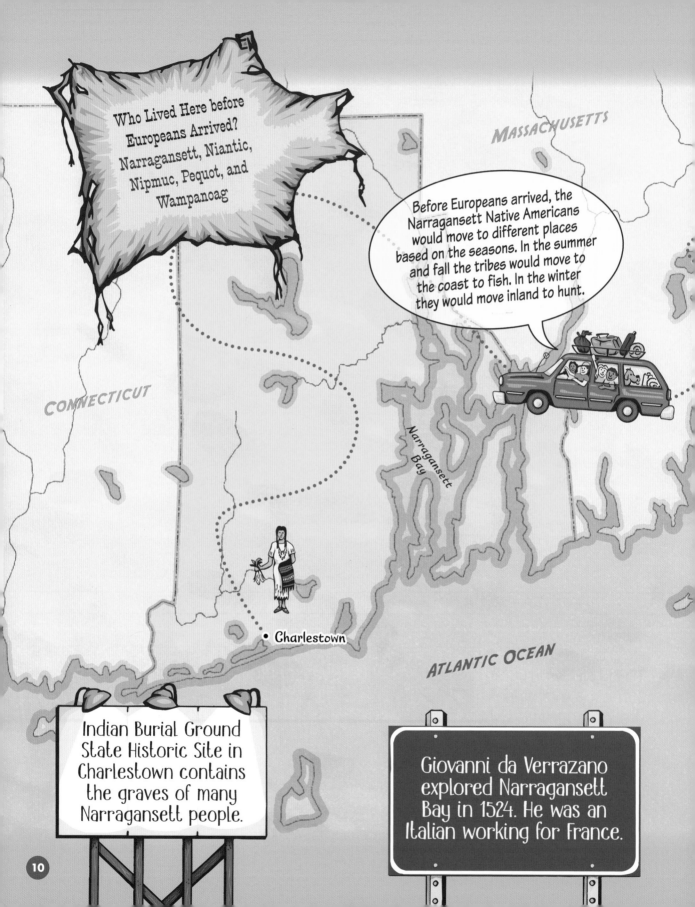

Who Lived Here before Europeans Arrived? Narragansett, Niantic, Nipmuc, Pequot, and Wampanoag

Before Europeans arrived, the Narragansett Native Americans would move to different places based on the seasons. In the summer and fall the tribes would move to the coast to fish. In the winter they would move inland to hunt.

MASSACHUSETTS

CONNECTICUT

Narragansett Bay

• Charlestown

ATLANTIC OCEAN

Indian Burial Ground State Historic Site in Charlestown contains the graves of many Narragansett people.

Giovanni da Verrazano explored Narragansett Bay in 1524. He was an Italian working for France.

NARRAGANSETT POWWOW IN CHARLESTOWN

I f you drive through Charlestown, stop by the oldest recorded powwow in North American history! The Narragansett Indian Tribe hosts this powwow in August every year. Visitors can taste traditional Narragansett food, listen to music, watch dances, and look at books and artwork.

Narragansett Native Americans have lived in Rhode Island for thousands of years. Each group has a sachem, or chief. When Europeans met the Narragansett peoples in 1524, they reported that the tribes had large populations.

Over time, more Europeans settled on the Narragansett's land. Eventually Europeans forced the Narragansett Native Americans off their land and onto **reservations**. Today, the Narragansett celebrate their culture and heritage through powwows.

You can listen to music at the Narragansett Powwow.

How did Rhode Island's first European settlers live? Just come to Opening Day at Smith's Castle in North Kingstown! You'll see people dressed in costumes from the 1600s. They demonstrate daily life on a **plantation**.

Roger Williams's trading post once stood here. Williams established a settlement called Providence Plantations. Narragansett Native Americans traded goods at his post.

Williams first lived in the Massachusetts Bay **Colony**. This colony didn't allow religious freedom. Williams left and founded Providence in 1636. He welcomed people of all faiths. Other settlers came to Aquidneck Island. Soon a new colony was formed. It was called Rhode Island and Providence Plantations.

Roger Williams was the founder of Rhode Island. A statue of him is located in Providence.

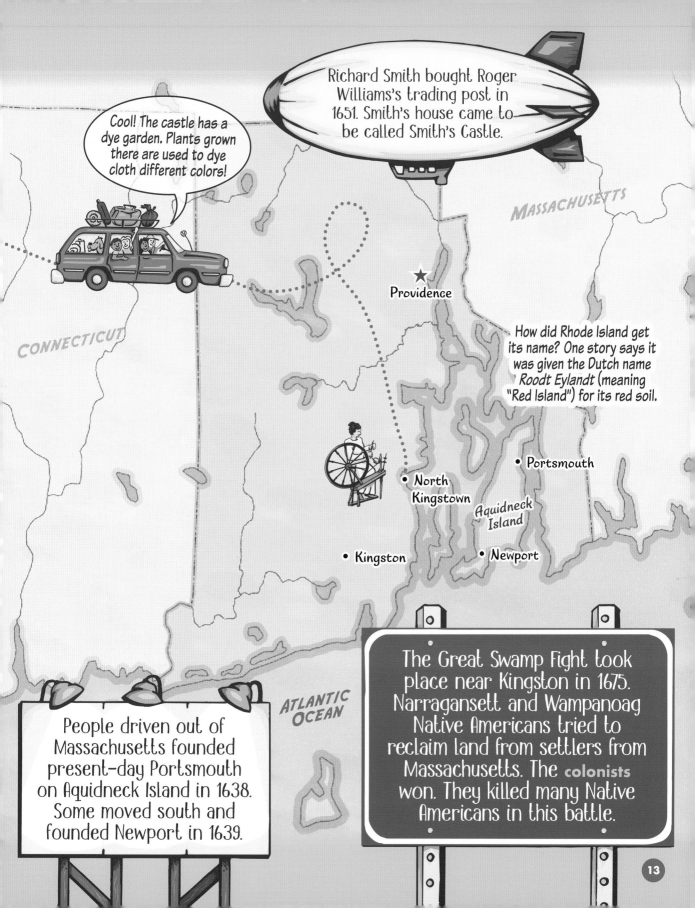

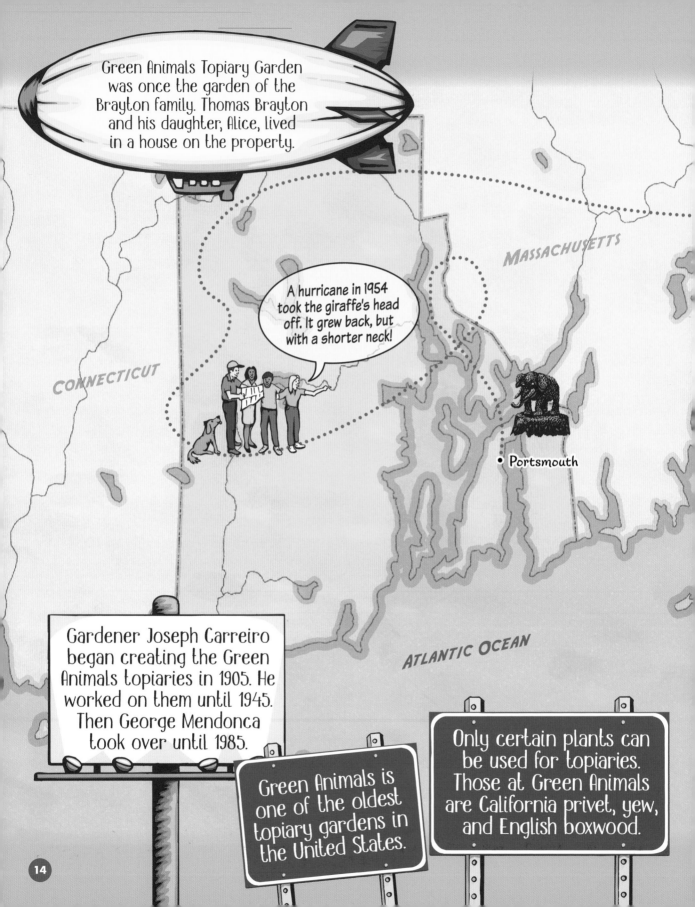

Green Animals Topiary Garden was once the garden of the Brayton family. Thomas Brayton and his daughter, Alice, lived in a house on the property.

A hurricane in 1954 took the giraffe's head off. It grew back, but with a shorter neck!

MASSACHUSETTS

CONNECTICUT

• Portsmouth

ATLANTIC OCEAN

Gardener Joseph Carreiro began creating the Green Animals topiaries in 1905. He worked on them until 1945. Then George Mendonca took over until 1985.

Green Animals is one of the oldest topiary gardens in the United States.

Only certain plants can be used for topiaries. Those at Green Animals are California privet, yew, and English boxwood.

GREEN ANIMALS TOPIARY GARDEN IN PORTSMOUTH

Here's a big, green elephant. There's a big, green giraffe. And look at that big, green teddy bear. You're exploring Green Animals Topiary Garden in Portsmouth!

Topiary is an art form. It's a type of sculpture. It involves trimming trees and bushes into shapes.

You'll see about 80 topiaries at Green Animals. Some are animals. And some are just shapes.

Topiary artists don't simply cut and trim. They also train branches. They carefully bend, weave, and tie them. It takes years to create a perfect shape!

Plants look like animals at the Green Animals Topiary Garden.

THE STATE CAPITOL IN PROVIDENCE

The state capitol in Providence has a massive dome. Stand beneath it and look up. It's full of huge paintings. One shows Roger Williams founding his new colony. Imagine how proud he'd be to see the capitol!

State government offices are inside this building. Rhode Island has three branches of government. One branch makes the state's laws. It's called the General Assembly. Another branch carries out the laws. The governor heads this branch. Judges make up the third branch. They apply the law to court cases. Then they decide whether laws have been broken.

Rhode Island has the second largest marble dome atop any state capitol. Only Minnesota's is larger.

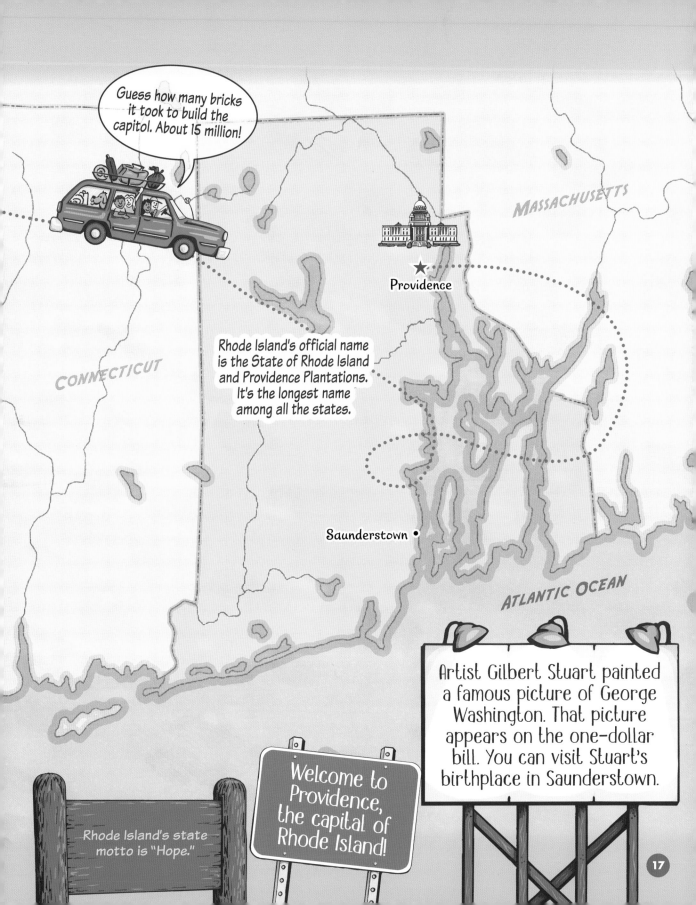

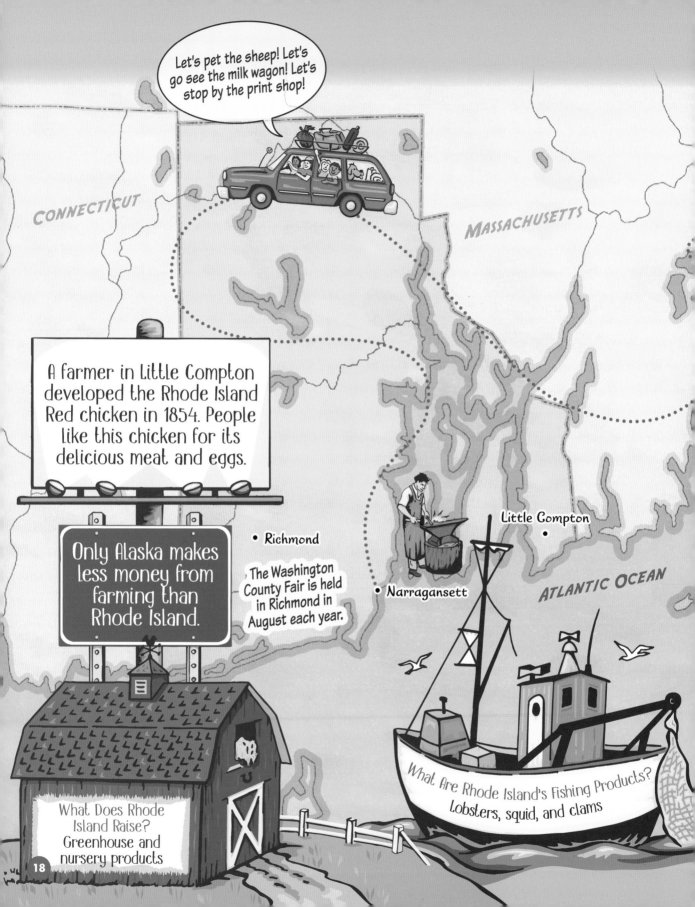

FARMING AT NARRAGANSETT'S SOUTH COUNTY MUSEUM

Stroll around the farmhouse and barn. People are busy with farm chores. Visit the carpenter's and blacksmith's shops. People there are hammering away.

You're touring South County Museum in Narragansett. It's a living history farm that's open from May through September. Everyone's dressed in 1800s clothing. And they're happy to chat with you. They tell you what farming was like long ago.

Most early settlers had farms. They grew much of what they needed. Today, trees and shrubs are important farm products in Rhode Island. Many farmers raise cows for their milk. Some grow potatoes, hay, and other crops. Others raise chickens that lay delicious eggs!

Kids can visit the chickens at South County Museum.

GASPÉE DAYS IN WARWICK

Bristol Men That Burned The Gaspee In 1772

Warwick's Gaspée Days is an annual spring festival. It has a colonial encampment, an arts and crafts festival, a parade, fireworks, and more. The event celebrates an exciting time in history!

Rhode Island was one of the 13 original colonies. The colonies were ruled by Great Britain. The colonists grew to hate Britain's high taxes.

Rhode Island colonists took action in 1772. They burned the British ship *Gaspée* in Narragansett Bay. This helped lead to the Revolutionary War (1775–1783). The colonies won! They became the first 13 U.S. states.

Don't forget to check out the Gaspeé Days parade.

Rhode Island was the 13th state to enter the Union. It joined on May 29, 1790.

Let's check out the Colonial Encampment. Colonial soldiers are camping out in Pawtuxet Park in Warwick!

Rhode Island College was founded in Warren in 1764. It moved to Providence in 1770. In 1804, it was renamed Brown University.

MASSACHUSETTS

★ Providence

• Warren

• Warwick

Coventry

Narragansett Bay

CONNECTICUT

Newport Harbor

ATLANTIC OCEAN

Nathanael Greene was an important general in the Revolutionary War. Greene's home still stands in Coventry.

A colony became a state when it ratified, or approved, the U.S. **Constitution**. Rhode Island was the last colony to give its approval.

In 1769, Rhode Islanders burned the British ship *Liberty* in Newport Harbor.

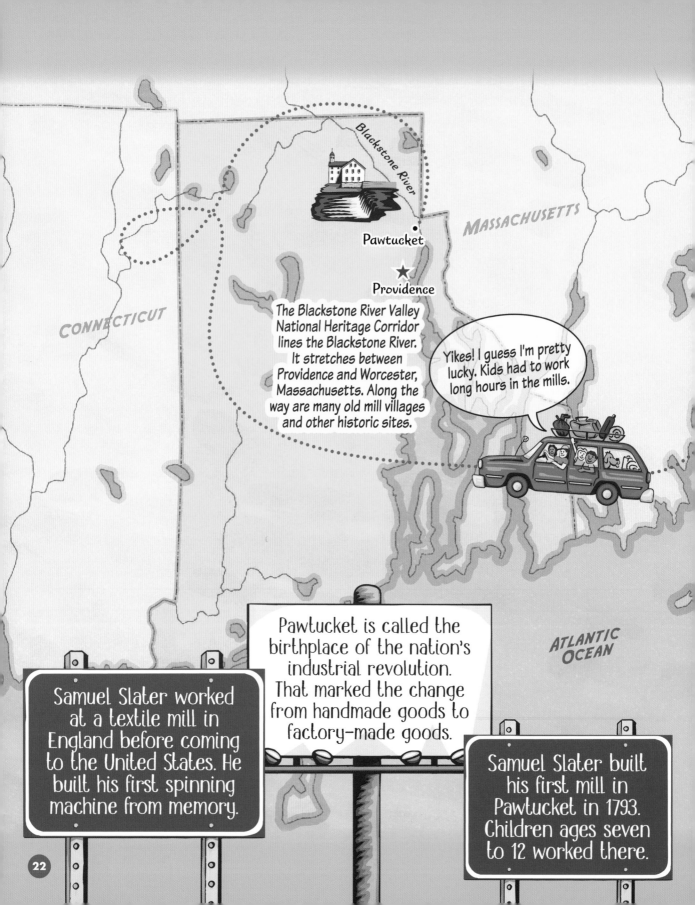

Blackstone River

Pawtucket

★ Providence

MASSACHUSETTS

CONNECTICUT

The Blackstone River Valley National Heritage Corridor lines the Blackstone River. It stretches between Providence and Worcester, Massachusetts. Along the way are many old mill villages and other historic sites.

Yikes! I guess I'm pretty lucky. Kids had to work long hours in the mills.

ATLANTIC OCEAN

Samuel Slater worked at a textile mill in England before coming to the United States. He built his first spinning machine from memory.

Pawtucket is called the birthplace of the nation's industrial revolution. That marked the change from handmade goods to factory-made goods.

Samuel Slater built his first mill in Pawtucket in 1793. Children ages seven to 12 worked there.

OLD SLATER MILL IN PAWTUCKET

The massive wheel begins to turn. The floor vibrates as machines clank. They spin raw cotton into thread and cloth. You're watching Slater Mill in action!

Samuel Slater built this mill in 1793. It was the country's first water-powered cotton mill. Water from the Blackstone River turns its wheel.

Dozens of mills once lined the Blackstone River. They made cotton and wool textiles, or cloth. Textiles became Rhode Island's leading **industry**.

Old Slater Mill National Historic Landmark in Pawtucket is a great place to visit. A mill workers' village surrounds the mill. Costumed villagers show you how the workers lived. The site has three buildings: the Slater Mill, Sylvanus Brown House, and the Wilkinson Mill.

Do you have what it takes to be a mill worker? Visit the Old Slater Mill and find out.

KENYON'S GRIST MILL IN USQUEPAUGH

Textile mills weren't Rhode Island's only mills. There were lots of grist mills, too. These were mills that ground grain. Corn or wheat was poured in. A huge stone ground up the grain. Then out came cornmeal or flour!

How did it all work? Just visit Kenyon's Grist Mill in Usquepaugh. It dates back to the early 1700s. It's still grinding grain the old-fashioned way.

Rhode Island has powerful factories now. Some make electrical equipment or computer products. Others make machines, tools, or plastics. Rhode Island is known for making jewelry, too.

Johnnycakes are a Rhode Island breakfast treat.

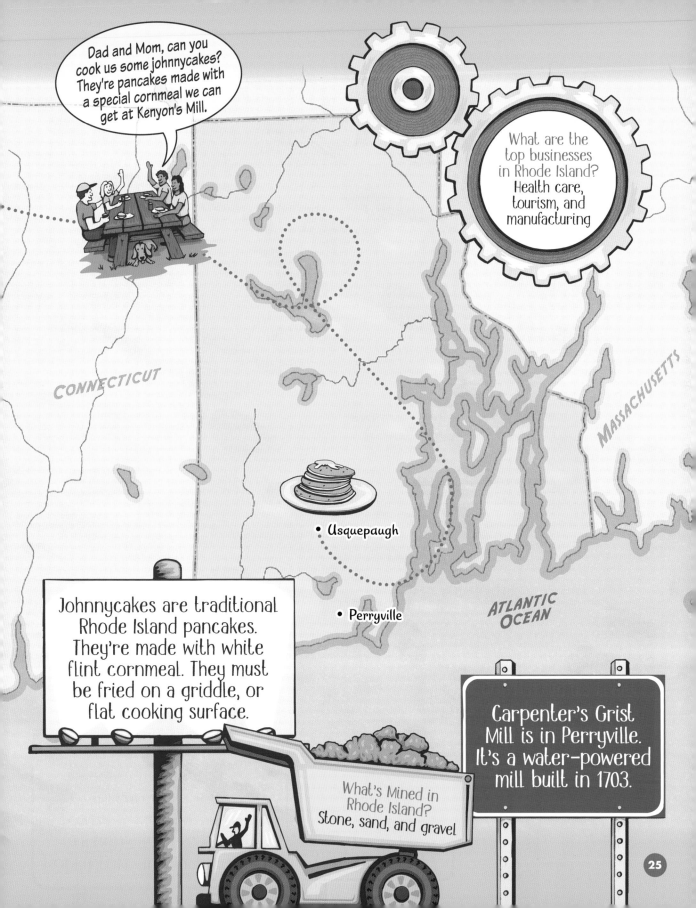

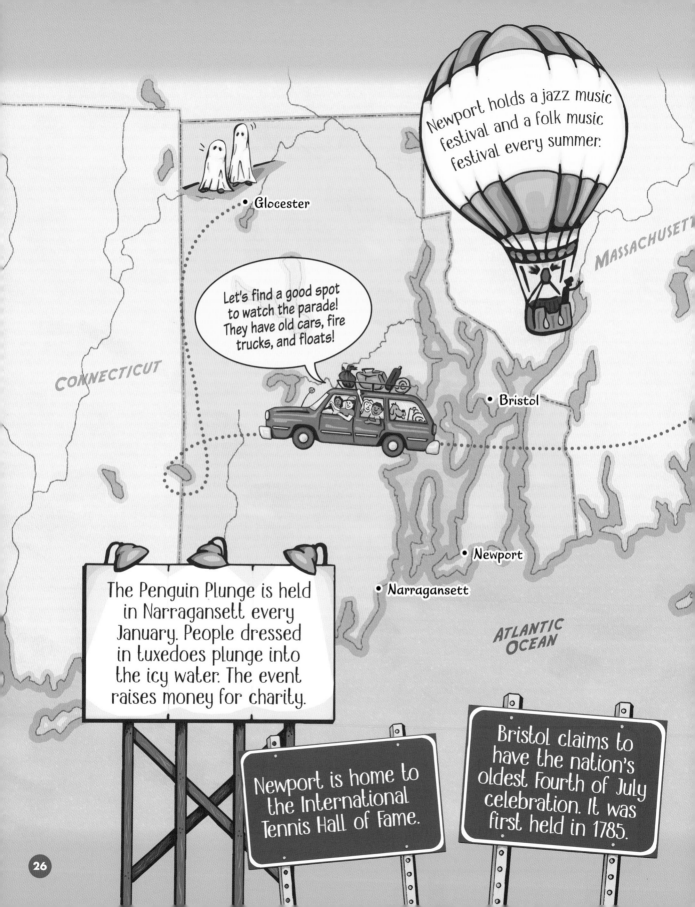

Newport holds a jazz music festival and a folk music festival every summer.

MASSACHUSETTS

Glocester

Let's find a good spot to watch the parade! They have old cars, fire trucks, and floats!

CONNECTICUT

Bristol

Newport

Narragansett

ATLANTIC OCEAN

The Penguin Plunge is held in Narragansett every January. People dressed in tuxedoes plunge into the icy water. The event raises money for charity.

Newport is home to the International Tennis Hall of Fame.

Bristol claims to have the nation's oldest Fourth of July celebration. It was first held in 1785.

THE ANCIENTS AND HORRIBLES PARADE

Check out the Ancients and Horribles Parade! It's held in Glocester every Fourth of July. People wear the wildest, ugliest outfits they can come up with. They decorate their cars, trucks, and bikes. Each vehicle looks really wacky, too.

Rhode Islanders find lots of ways to have fun. They hold parades, sailboat races, and fishing contests. They attend seafood festivals and clambakes. There's plenty to do along the shore. People enjoy swimming, boating, and fishing.

The first Ancients and Horribles Parade was in 1926.

THE FRENCH CANADIANS OF WOONSOCKET

Stroll through a millworker's living room. Hear workers chat in a textile mill. Visit a school classroom from the 1920s.

You're at Woonsocket's Museum of Work and Culture. It's all about the city's French Canadian **immigrants**. You can walk right through the displays!

French Canadians are Woonsocket's largest **ethnic** group. Thousands of them arrived in the 1800s. They came from Canada's Quebec province. They went to work in Woonsocket's mills.

Many other immigrant groups moved to Rhode Island. They came from Italy, Portugal, Sweden, and Poland.

Rhode Island textile mills create fabric.

In 1900, about three out of 10 Rhode Islanders were born outside the United States.

Wow! Woonsocket's mills made cotton cloth, rubber, and various machines.

In 2016, 1,056,426 people lived in Rhode Island. It's the 43rd-largest state by population.

The Woonsocket Rubber Company made rubber boots and shoes. It was the country's largest rubber factory in the 1890s!

Woonsocket's Bailey Wringer Company made an early type of washing machine.

Woonsocket

MASSACHUSETTS

★ Providence

Cranston •

Warwick

CONNECTICUT

ATLANTIC OCEAN

POPULATION OF LARGEST CITIES
Providence.....................179,207
Warwick.........................81,699
Cranston........................81,073

CONNECTICUT

MASSACHUSETTS

Let's visit The Breakers at Christmastime. We'll see their huge Christmas tree!

Rhode Island's first library was founded in 1700 in Newport by Thomas Bray.

• Newport

ATLANTIC OCEAN

Cliff Walk is a high seaside walking path in Newport. It passes many mansions.

The late 1800s are sometimes called the Gilded Age, or the Golden Age. It's a time when many industry leaders made huge fortunes. The Newport mansions reflect this time.

Newport's Touro Synagogue was built in 1763. It's the oldest Jewish house of worship in the United States.

NEWPORT MANSIONS

Newport is home to some beautiful, old mansions! You can tour several of them. Wealthy people built the mansions in the late 1800s. Many of the owners lived in New York most of the year. The Newport mansions were just their summer homes!

Three mansions visitors can see are The Breakers, The Elms, and Marble House. People call The Breakers the crown jewel of Newport. It has 70 rooms and more than 200 windows. Visitors can also tour The Breakers's underground tunnel, boiler room, and basement. Each mansion in Newport is beautifully decorated!

Cornelius Vanderbilt II hired an architect to design The Breakers in 1893.

THE FOOLS' RULES REGATTA IN JAMESTOWN

Boom! The cannon fires, and people start to work. They have two hours to build their sailboats. They might use doghouses or sandboxes. They might use car parts or chicken cages. They name their boats, and then the race begins. It's the Fools' Rules **Regatta** in Jamestown!

This is a race for really silly boats. Rhode Island has many serious sailboat races, too. It also has many ties with the U.S. Navy.

A **torpedo** factory opened on Goat Island in 1906. Rhode Island built warships during World War I (1914–1918). The state was also busy during World War II (1939–1945). Thousands of navy troops trained there.

Anyone can participate in the Fools' Rules Regatta.

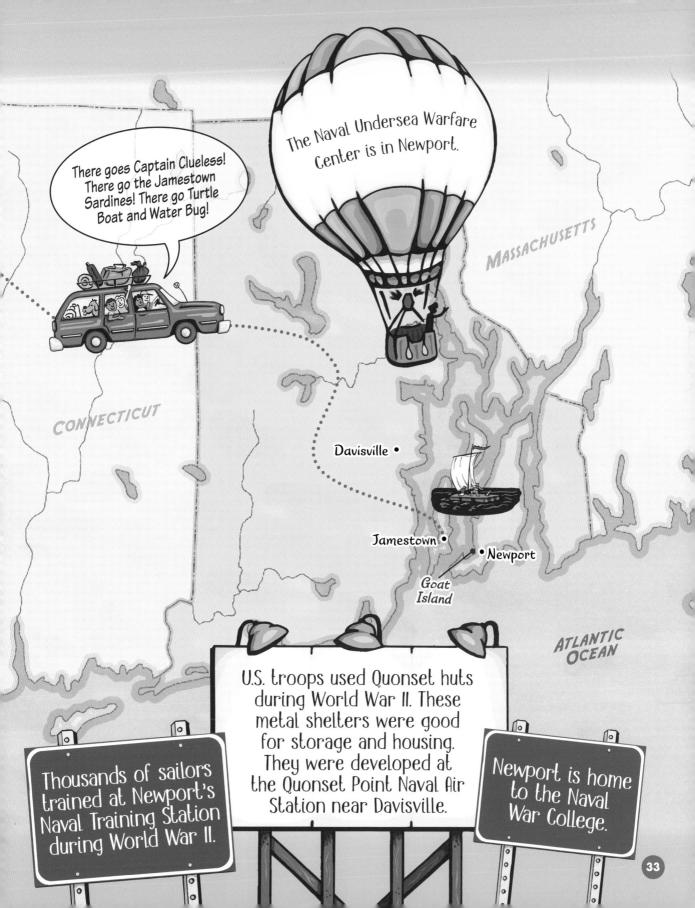

Looff Carousel is in Crescent Park in East Providence. It has 66 hand-carved figures.

MASSACHUSETTS

Pawtucket

East Providence

We heard an old tale about a horse. It used to pull the carousel around. Can it be true?

CONNECTICUT

The Flying Horse Carousel is in the Watch Hill section of Westerly.

Westerly

ATLANTIC OCEAN

Slater Park Carousel is in Pawtucket. Visitors can ride horses, dogs, a camel, or a giraffe!

People need to be under five feet and 100 pounds to ride the Flying Horse Carousel.

Carousel artist Charles Looff carved the carousel animals in Pawtucket and East Providence.

WESTERLY'S FLYING HORSE CAROUSEL

Whee! You're riding a carousel, or merry-go-round. And you're not just moving up and down. You're sailing through the air! You're riding the Flying Horse Carousel in Westerly. It dates from the 1870s.

These carousel horses are hand-carved from wood. Their manes and tails are real horse hair. They wear leather saddles. And their eyes seem to sparkle! They're made of a stone called agate.

Why is this called the Flying Horse Carousel? The horses aren't attached to the floor. They only hang from above. When the carousel turns, the horses swing outward. The faster the ride, the farther they swing. They really seem to fly!

Choose a horse and hold on tight! The horses on this carousel soar through the air.

What are the six New England states? *See page 5 for the answer.*

What are the largest cities on Aquidneck Island? *Page 6 has the answer.*

When did the Great Swamp Fight take place? *See page 13 for the answer.*

What are some plants that can be used in topiaries? *Look on page 14 for the answer.*

What was Brown University once called? *Page 21 has the answer.*

What are johnnycakes? *Turn to page 25 for the answer.*

When was Newport's Touro Synagogue built? *Look on page 30 for the answer.*

Who carved the carousel animals in Pawtucket and East Providence? *Turn to page 34 for the answer.*

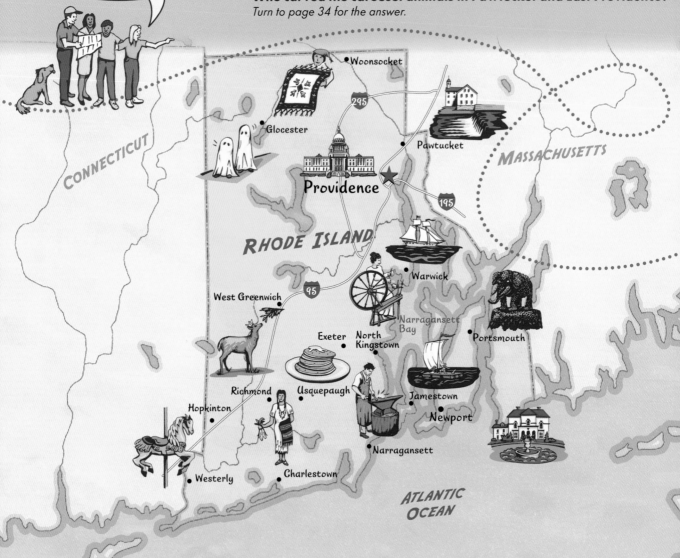

STATE SYMBOLS

State bird: Rhode Island Red (a chicken)

State drink: Coffee milk

State fish: Striped bass

State flagship: Continental schooner *Providence*

State flower: Violet

State fruit: Rhode Island greening (an apple)

State mineral: Bowenite

State rock: Cumberlandite

State shell: Quahaug

State tree: Red maple

State yacht: *Courageous*

STATE SONG

"RHODE ISLAND'S IT FOR ME"
Words by Charlie Hall, music by Maria Day

I've been to every state we have,
and I think that I'm inclined to say
that Rhody stole my heart:
You can keep the forty-nine.

Herring gulls that dot the sky,
blue waves that paint the rocks,
waters rich with Neptune's life,
the boats that line the docks,
I see the lighthouse flickering
to help the sailors see.
There's a place for everyone:
Rhode Island's it for me.

Chorus:
Rhode Island, oh, Rhode Island
surrounded by the sea.
Some people roam the earth
   for home;
Rhode Island's it for me.

I love the fresh October days,
the buzz of College Hill,
art that moves an eye to tear,
a jeweler's special skill.
Icicles refract the sun,
snow falling gracefully.
Some search for a place
   that's warm:
Rhode Island's it for me.

(Chorus)

The skyline piercing Providence,
the State House dome so rare,
residents who speak their minds;
no longer unaware!
Roger Williams would be proud
to see his "colony,"
so don't sell short this
   precious port:
Rhode Island's it for me.

That was a great trip! We have traveled all over Rhode Island! There are a few places we didn't have time for, though. Next time, we plan to visit Roger Williams Park Zoo in Providence. Visitors can see more than 1,000 animals, including giraffes and snow leopards. Kids learn about various endangered animals and what they can do to help them.

State flag

State seal

FAMOUS PEOPLE

Burnside, Ambrose Everett (1824–1881), Civil War general, former governor of Rhode Island

Cohan, George M. (1878–1942), entertainer

Colasanto, Nicholas (1924–1985), actor and director

Gray, Robert (1755–1806), sea captain

Hackett, Bobby (1915–1976), jazz musician

Hasselbeck, Elisabeth (1977–), talk show host, reality television star

Howe, Julia Ward (1819–1910), writer and reformer

Hussey, Ruth (1914–2005), actor

Hutchinson, Anne (1591–1643), religious leader

Kinnell, Galway (1927–2004), poet

Lajoie, Napoleon (1874–1959), baseball player

Lovecraft, H. P. (1890–1937), author

Macaulay, David (1946–), children's author and illustrator

Massasoit (ca. 1580–1661), Wampanoag Native American chief

Perry, Matthew C. (1794–1858), U.S. Navy officer

Perry, Oliver Hazard (1785–1819), U.S. Navy officer and war hero

Slater, Samuel (1768–1835), founder of the U.S. textile industry

Stuart, Gilbert Charles (1755–1828), painter

Vieira, Meredith (1953–), talk show host, news anchor

Williams, Roger (ca. 1603–1683), founder of Rhode Island

Woodcock, Leonard (1911–2001), labor leader

WORDS TO KNOW

clambake (KLAM-bake) a beach party where clams are cooked

colonists (KOL-uh-nists) people who settle a new land for their home country

colony (KOL-uh-nee) a land settled and governed by another country

constitution (kon-stuh-TOO-shuhn) the basic set of ideas and laws for a country or state

ethnic (ETH-nik) relating to a person's race or nationality

immigrants (IM-uh-gruhnts) people who move to another country

industry (IN-duh-stree) a type of business

mainland (MAYN-luhnd) land that makes up the main part of a state or country

plantation (plan-TAY-shuhn) a large farm that raises mainly one crop

regatta (ri-GAT-uh) a boat race

reservations (rez-ur-VAY-shuns) areas of land set aside for special use, such as for Native Americans

torpedo (tor-PEE-doh) a missile that's fired underwater

tradition (truh-DISH-uhn) a long-held custom

TO LEARN MORE

IN THE LIBRARY

Burgan, Michael. *Rhode Island*. New York, NY: Children's Press, 2015.

Felix, Rebecca. *What's Great about Rhode Island?* Minneapolis, MN: Lerner, 2015.

Furgang, Adam. *Rhode Island: Past and Present*. New York, NY: Rosen Central, 2011.

Roza, Greg. *The Colony of Rhode Island*. New York: PowerKids, 2015.

ON THE WEB
Visit our Web site for links about Rhode Island:

childsworld.com/links

Note to Parents, Teachers, and Librarians: We routinely verify our Web links to make sure they are safe and active sites. So encourage your readers to check them out!

PLACES TO VISIT OR CONTACT
Rhode Island Historical Society

rihs.org
52 Power Street
Providence, RI 02906
401/331-6630
For more information about the history of Rhode Island

Visit Rhode Island

visitrhodeisland.com
315 Iron Horse Way #101
Providence, RI 02903
401/298-9100
For more information about traveling in Rhode Island

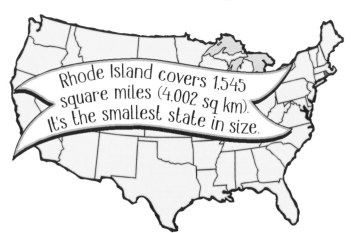

Rhode Island covers 1,545 square miles (4,002 sq km). It's the smallest state in size.

INDEX

Bye, Ocean State. We had a great time. We'll come back soon!